Informing the legislative debate since 1914 _____

# The LIHEAP Formula

**Libby Perl**
Specialist in Housing Policy

May 21, 2014

Congressional Research Service

7-5700

www.crs.gov

RL33275

# Summary

The Low Income Home Energy Assistance Program (LIHEAP) provides funds to states, the District of Columbia, U.S. territories and commonwealths, and Indian tribal organizations (collectively referred to as grantees) primarily to help low-income households pay home energy expenses. The LIHEAP statute provides for two types of funding: regular funds (sometimes referred to as block grant funds) and emergency contingency funds. Regular funds are allocated to grantees based on a formula, while emergency contingency funds may be released to one or more grantees at the discretion of the Secretary of the Department of Health and Human Services based on emergency need. This report focuses on the way in which regular funds are distributed.

Regular LIHEAP funds are allocated to the states according to a formula that has a long and complicated history. (Tribes and territories receive funds through set asides.) In 1980, Congress created the predecessor program to LIHEAP, the Low Income Energy Assistance Program (LIEAP), as part of the Crude Oil Windfall Profits Tax Act (P.L. 96-223). Because Congress was particularly concerned with the high costs of heating, funds under LIEAP were distributed according to a multi-step formula that benefitted cold-weather states. In 1981, Congress enacted LIHEAP as part of the Omnibus Budget Reconciliation Act (P.L. 97-35), replacing LIEAP. However, the LIHEAP statute specified that states would continue to receive the same percentage of regular funds that they did under the LIEAP formula (this is sometimes referred to as the "old" LIHEAP formula).

When Congress reauthorized LIHEAP in 1984 as part of the Human Services Reauthorization Act (P.L. 98-558), it changed the program's formula by requiring the use of more recent population and energy data and requiring that HHS consider both heating and cooling costs of low-income households (a change from what had largely been a focus on the need for heating assistance). The effect of these changes meant that, in general, some funding would be shifted from cold-weather states to warm-weather states. To prevent a dramatic shift of funds, Congress added two "hold-harmless" provisions to the formula. The percentage of funds that states receive under the formula enacted in 1984 is sometimes referred to as the "new" formula.

The result of these provisions is a current law, three-tiered formula, the application of which depends on the amount of regular funds that Congress appropriates. When appropriations are at or below the equivalent of a hypothetical FY1984 appropriation of $1.975 billion, states receive the "old" formula percentage of funds. If appropriations exceed this level, then funds are allocated according to the "new" formula percentage of funds, with certain states held harmless at the *level* of funds they would have received at an appropriation of $1.975 billion in FY1984. Finally, when appropriations are at or above $2.25 billion, there is a second hold-harmless provision in place, a hold-harmless *rate* that ensures that certain states receive a set percentage of funds.

For many years after the enactment of the "new" LIHEAP formula, appropriations did not exceed the equivalent of an FY1984 appropriation of $1.975 billion, so funds were distributed according to the "old" formula percentages. However, in FY2006, and in FY2009 through FY2014, regular fund appropriations have ranged from $2.5 billion to $4.5 billion, and the "new" formula has been incorporated into the way in which funds are distributed to the states. In FY2015, the President's budget proposal would incorporate the "new" LIHEAP formula into the fund distribution. For estimated allocations to the states, see Table C-1.

# Contents

## Appendixes

## Contacts

# Introduction

The Low Income Home Energy Assistance Program (LIHEAP) is a block grant program administered by the Department of Health and Human Services (HHS) under which the federal government gives annual grants to states, the District of Columbia, U.S. territories and commonwealths, and Indian tribal organizations to operate multi-component home energy assistance programs for needy households.[1] Established in 1981 by Title XXVI of P.L. 97-35, the Omnibus Budget Reconciliation Act, LIHEAP has been reauthorized and amended a number of times, most recently in 2005, when P.L. 109-58, the Energy Policy Act, authorized annual regular LIHEAP funds at $5.1 billion per year from FY2005 through FY2007.[2]

The federal LIHEAP statute has very broad guidelines, with many decisions regarding the program's operation made by the states. Recipients may be helped with their heating and cooling costs, receive crisis assistance, have weatherizing expenses paid, or receive other aid designed to reduce their home energy needs. Households with incomes up to 150% of the federal poverty income guidelines or, if greater, 60% of the state median income, are federally eligible for LIHEAP benefits. States may adopt lower income limits, but no household with income below 110% of the poverty guidelines may be considered ineligible. The most recent HHS data show that an estimated 7.4 million households received winter heating or winter crisis assistance in FY2009 (the largest share of LIHEAP funds pay for heating assistance).[3]

The LIHEAP statute provides for two types of program funding: regular funds—sometimes referred to as block grant funds—and emergency contingency funds. Regular funds are allotted to states on the basis of the LIHEAP statutory formula, which was enacted as part of the Human Services Reauthorization Act of 1984 (P.L. 98-558).[4] The way in which regular funds are allocated to states depends on the amount of funds appropriated by Congress. The second type of LIHEAP funds, emergency contingency funds, may be released and allotted to one or more states at the discretion of the President and the Secretary of HHS.[5] The funds may be released at any point in the fiscal year to meet additional home energy assistance needs created by a natural disaster or other emergency.[6]

The remainder of this report discusses only the history and methods of distributing regular LIHEAP funds to the state. Funds for tribes are included in each state's formula allocations and are distributed at the state level based on eligible tribal members. Territories receive funds separately as a percentage set aside of regular funds, so neither tribes nor territories are included in the formula discussion.

---

[1] For additional information on LIHEAP, see CRS Report RL31865, *LIHEAP: Program and Funding*, by Libby Perl.

[2] LIHEAP is codified at 42 U.S.C. §§8621-8630.

[3] U.S. Department of Health and Human Services, Administration for Children and Families, *LIHEAP Home Energy Notebook for Fiscal Year 2009*, September 2011, p. 30.

[4] The formula section is codified at 42 U.S.C. §8623.

[5] Depending on how Congress appropriates them, contingency funds may remain available for distribution in more than one fiscal year or they may expire with the fiscal year for which they were appropriated.

[6] The statutory definition of emergency includes a significant home energy supply shortage or disruption, a significant increase in the cost of home energy, a significant increase in home energy disconnections, a significant increase in participation in a public benefit program, a significant increase in unemployment, or an event meeting such criteria as the Secretary determines to be appropriate. 42 U.S.C. §8622.

# Predecessor Programs to LIHEAP

The mid- to late-1970s, a time marked by rapidly rising fuel prices, also marked the beginning of federal energy assistance funding for low-income households. The first national program to help low-income households was created in early 1975 to assist families with energy conservation primarily through home weatherization. This assistance was provided through a new Emergency Energy Conservation Program (EECP), enacted as part of the Headstart, Economic Opportunity, and Community Partnership Act of 1974 (P.L. 93-644). The funds were administered by the Community Services Administration (CSA), the successor agency to the Office of Economic Opportunity, which was responsible for many of the programs created as part of the 1964 war on poverty. Beginning in 1977, funds were also made available through the CSA to help families directly pay for fuel (as opposed to weatherization expenses) via a variety of programs. Each of these programs had in common a focus on the need for heating assistance (versus cooling assistance).

Congress continued to appropriate funds for energy assistance programs through FY1980, at which point a new program, the Low Income Energy Assistance Program (LIEAP), was enacted as part of the Crude Oil Windfall Profits Tax Act of 1980 (P.L. 96-223). LIEAP, which was administered by the Department of Health and Human Services (HHS), was funded for one year, FY1981, before the creation of LIHEAP. Like the CSA programs, LIEAP emphasized heating over cooling needs. This preference was reflected in both the CSA program formulas and the LIEAP set of formulas, which used variables that benefitted cold-weather states to determine how funds would be distributed. The LIEAP set of formulas continues to have relevance for the way in which LIHEAP funds are distributed. This section of the report describes these predecessor programs to LIHEAP and their distribution formulas.

## Community Services Administration Energy Assistance Programs

On January 4, 1975, President Ford signed into law the Headstart, Economic Opportunity, and Community Partnership Act of 1974 (P.L. 93-644), which contained funds for a new program, called the Emergency Energy Conservation Program (EECP). The program was to be administered by the Community Services Administration (CSA), and its purpose was

> to enable low-income individuals and families, including the elderly and the near poor, to participate in energy conservation programs designed to lessen the impact of the high cost of energy ... and to reduce ... energy consumption.

The law governing EECP listed a number of eligible activities in which states could participate, including energy conservation and education programs; weatherization assistance; loans and grants for the purchase of energy conservation technologies; alternative fuel supplies; and fuel voucher and stamp programs. Despite the variety of activities that could be funded through the program, the first CSA funding notice regarding the program limited eligible activities to "winterizing" homes and to giving emergency assistance "to prevent hardship or danger to health due to utility shutoff or lack of fuel."[7] During the four years the EECP was funded, the majority of funds were used for weatherization expenses.[8]

EECP funds were distributed to states via a formula that benefitted those states with high heating costs. One formula variable in particular, a measure of "coldness" called heating degree days, benefitted cold-weather states. Heating degree days measure the extent to which a day's average temperature falls below 65° Fahrenheit. For example, a day with an average temperature of 50° results in a measure of 15 heating degree days. Because heating degree days are higher in cold-weather states, including the heating degree day variable in a formula favors states with greater heating needs. Squaring the heating degree days magnifies this effect.[9] The EECP formula took the number of population-weighted heating degree days in each state, squared them, and multiplied the result by the number of households in poverty that owned their homes to determine how funds would be allocated.[10] The CSA acknowledged the emphasis on heating needs in its formula, stating that the FY1975 allocation "was heavily weighted to the coldest areas."[11] In the three fiscal years that followed the first appropriation for the EECP, from FY1976 through FY1978, the CSA changed somewhat the way in which it allocated funds to the states; however, the factors continued to favor cold-weather states through use of either heating degree days or heating degree days squared.[12]

The first year that Congress specifically appropriated funds for direct assistance to help low-income households (those at or below 125% of poverty) pay their energy costs (instead of funds that went primarily for weatherization and conservation activities) was FY1977. The FY1977 Supplemental Appropriations Act (P.L. 95-26) provided $200 million for a Special Crisis Intervention Program to be administered by CSA. States could use funds to make direct payments to fuel providers on behalf of low-income families lacking the financial resources to pay their energy bills. The CSA directed states to target households where utilities had been shut off (or were threatened with shut off) or who could prove "dire financial need" as the result of paying large energy bills.[13] Although the law did not reserve funds exclusively for heating costs, the way in which funds were allocated to the states emphasized heating need. Funds were distributed to the states based on a formula that used (1) heating degree days squared, (2) the number of households in poverty, (3) the number of persons above age 65 with incomes below 125% of poverty, and (4) the relative cost of fuel in the region.[14] Congress again appropriated $200 million

---

[7] Community Services Administration, "Character and Scope of Specific Community Action Programs: Emergency Energy Conservation Program," *Federal Register*, vol. 40, no. 145, July 28, 1975, p. 31603.

[8] See, for example, House Appropriations Committee, report to accompany H.R. 4877, the FY1977 Supplemental Appropriations Act, 95th Cong., 1st sess., H.Rept. 95-68, March 11, 1977: "The funds in this program are used primarily to purchase materials to insulate the homes of low-income families."

[9] For example, if a southern state experiences 700 heating degree days in a year and a northern state experiences 7,000, the northern state has 10 times as many heating degree days as the southern state. However, if both numbers are squared, the northern state has 100 times as many heating degree days as the southern state.

[10] Community Services Administration, "Emergency Energy Conservation Program: Submission of Funding Plans," *Federal Register*, vol. 41, no. 208, October 27, 1976, p. 47096.

[11] Ibid.

[12] Ibid., pp. 47096-47097.

[13] Community Services Administration, "Special Crisis Intervention Program: General Information, Application Procedures, and Post Grant Requirements," *Federal Register*, vol. 42, no. 125, June 29, 1977, p. 33240.

[14] The formula was described in the Senate Appropriations Committee report to accompany H.R. 4877, the FY1977 Supplemental Appropriations Act, 95th Cong., 1st sess., S.Rept. 95-64, March 24, 1977. The CSA implemented this formula, which it described in guidance to the states. See the *Federal Register*, Ibid.

for crisis intervention in both FY1978 and FY1979.[15] In FY1978, funds were available to households with the need for assistance as the result of an energy-related emergency such as lack of fuel, a natural disaster, fuel shortages, and widespread unemployment.[16] In FY1979, funds were made available to assist families facing "substantially increased energy costs and/or life- or health-threatening situations caused by winter-related energy emergencies."[17]

In FY1980, Congress appropriated a total of $1.6 billion for energy assistance. Of this amount, $400 million was appropriated for the Energy Crisis Assistance Program (ECAP, a CSA program similar to the Special Crisis Intervention Program) through two separate appropriations.[18] The remainder, $1.2 billion, was appropriated as part of the FY1980 Department of the Interior Appropriations Act (P.L. 96-126) to the Department of Health, Education, and Welfare (HEW, the predecessor to HHS) for cash assistance and crisis intervention due to high energy costs. This appropriation to HEW is sometimes referred to as Low Income Supplemental Energy Allowances. Of this $1.2 billion, $400 million was to be distributed specifically to recipients of Supplemental Security Income (SSI). The rest of the funds appropriated to HEW, approximately $800 million, as well as the ECAP funds, were distributed to states on the basis of three factors: heating degree days squared, the number of households below 125% of poverty, and the difference in home heating energy expenditures between 1978 and 1979. The formula used to distribute the $400 million for SSI recipients used these same factors but also included the number of SSI recipients in each state relative to the national total.

**Table 1. Factors Used in Select Energy Assistance Formulas, FY1975-FY1980**

| Emergency Energy Conservation Program:[a] FY1975 (P.L. 93-644) | Special Crisis Intervention Program:[b] FY1977 (P.L. 95-26) | Low Income Supplemental Energy Allowances:[c] FY1980 (P.L. 96-126) |
|---|---|---|
| (Heating degree days)$^2$ | (Heating degree days)$^2$ | (Heating degree days)$^2$ |
| Number of homeowners in poverty | Number of households in poverty | Number of households below 125% of poverty |
| | Number of persons over age 65 with income less than 125% of poverty | Difference in home heating expenditures between 1978 and 1979 |
| | Relative cost of fuel | |

**Sources:** For the formula under P.L. 93-644, see Community Services Administration, "Emergency Energy Conservation Program: Submission of Funding Plans," *Federal Register*, vol. 41, no. 208, October 27, 1976, p. 47096. For the formula under P.L. 95-26, see Senate Appropriations Committee, report to accompany H.R. 4877, the FY1977 Supplemental Appropriations Act, 95th Congress, 1st session, S.Rept. 95-64, March 24, 1977. The formula for P.L. 96-126 is contained within the law.

---

[15] Funds were appropriated through the FY1978 Supplemental Appropriations Act (P.L. 95-240) and in FY1979 through a continuing resolution (P.L. 95-482). In FY1978, Congress called the program Emergency Energy Assistance Program and in FY1979 called it the Crisis Intervention Program (excluding the word "Special" from the title).

[16] Community Services Administration, "Emergency Energy Conservation Program: Funding Requirements for Emergency Energy Assistance Program," *Federal Register*, vol. 43, no. 46, March 8, 1978, p. 9476.

[17] Community Services Administration, "Emergency Energy Conservation Program: Fiscal Year 1979 Crisis Intervention Program," *Federal Register*, vol. 43, no. 250, December 28, 1978, pp. 60466-60467.

[18] Congress appropriated $250 million for ECAP as part of an FY1980 Continuing Resolution (P.L. 96-123, referencing the FY1980 Departments of Labor, Health and Human Services and Education Appropriations bill, H.R. 4389), and appropriated an additional $150 million as part of the Department of the Interior Appropriations Act (P.L. 96-126).

a. Of the funds appropriated for the Emergency Energy Conservation Program, 90% were distributed via the formula, while the remaining 10% were divided among the 12 coldest states as measured by heating degree days. The formula involved multiplying heating degree days squared by the number of homeowners in poverty to arrive at the percentage share for each state.

b. The Special Crisis Intervention Program did not specify a weight for each of the four variables used to determine allocations.

c. The Low Income Supplemental Energy Allowances arrived at states' shares of funds through the formula ½ (heating degree days$^2$ * number of households below 125% of poverty) + ½ (difference in home heating expenditures between 1978 and 1980). Of the $1.6 billion appropriated for energy assistance in FY1980, $400 million was set aside for SSI recipients. The formula to distribute those funds was ⅓ (heating degree days$^2$ * number of households below 125% of poverty) + ⅓ (difference in home heating expenditures between 1978 and 1979) + ⅓ (SSI recipients in each state relative to the national total).

# The Low Income Energy Assistance Program (LIEAP) Formula

In April 1980, Congress replaced the patchwork energy assistance programs of the late 1970s with one program, the Low Income Energy Assistance Program (LIEAP). LIEAP, the direct predecessor program to LIHEAP, was established as part of the Crude Oil Windfall Profits Tax Act of 1980 (P.L. 96-223). The program was introduced in the Senate as the Home Energy Assistance Act (S. 1724) and was incorporated into H.R. 3919, the bill that would become the Crude Oil Windfall Profits Tax Act, on the Senate floor.[19] Like the energy assistance programs of the late 1970s such as the Special Crisis Intervention Program and the Low Income Supplemental Energy Allowances, LIEAP allocated funds to states in order to help low-income households pay their home energy costs. Also like these predecessor programs, LIEAP allocated funds to states using a method that put more emphasis on the heating needs of cold-weather states than it did on cooling needs.

The formula developed under LIEAP continues to be relevant in several ways: (1) it has been used to distribute LIHEAP funds as recently as FY2007, (2) the percentage shares of funds that states received continue to be the benchmark for the way in which states are held harmless under the current LIHEAP formula, and (3) from FY2009 through FY2012, Congress has distributed the bulk of LIHEAP funds using the LIEAP formula percentages (for more information, see **Appendix C**). As a result, the variables used are important in understanding the current formula and the way in which it is used to distribute funds.

Ultimately, Congress developed the LIEAP formula through two different laws: P.L. 96-223, the law that authorized LIEAP, and P.L. 96-369, a continuing resolution enacted six months later. The following two subsections describe the elements of the formula developed through each.

## *Formula Under P.L. 96-223*

The formula developed as part of S. 1724, and subsequently incorporated into P.L. 96-223, reflected, in part, the concern that the problem of rising energy costs were "most critical in areas with high home heating costs."[20] The formula for LIEAP arose from a Senate compromise over three different proposals. The debate centered around the degree to which heating should be

---

[19] "Windfall Profits Tax." In *CQ Almanac 1979*, 35th ed., 609-32 (Washington, DC: Congressional Quarterly, 1980) http://library.cqpress.com/cqalmanac/cqal79-1184031.

[20] Senate Committee on Labor and Human Resources, *Home Energy Assistance Act*, report to accompany S. 1724, 96th Cong., 1st sess., S.Rept. 96-378, October 25, 1979, p. 12.

emphasized over energy expenditures generally. Some Members wanted a formula that accounted for all energy uses and was not based solely on geographic location,[21] while others saw the program's purpose as solely to provide heating assistance.[22] The debate on the Senate floor was, at times, contentious, with Senator Edmund Muskie (ME) resolved to filibuster in order to support the heating needs of northern states.[23] Primarily at issue was the measure of heating degree days, particularly the extent to which they would be weighted and whether they would be squared.

Under the final compromise LIEAP formula in P.L. 96-223, states received funds under one of four different alternatives used to measure home energy need, depending on which one benefitted a state the most. Three of the four options contained different combinations of several formula factors: residential energy expenditures; heating degree days or heating degree days squared; and the number of low-income households in the state.

- Under the first formula alternative, 50% of the allocation was based on residential energy expenditures and 50% on heating degree days squared multiplied by the number of households at or below the Bureau of Labor Statistics (BLS) lower living standard.[24]

- Under the second formula alternative, 25% of the allocation was based on residential energy expenditures and 75% based on heating degree days squared multiplied by the number of households at or below the BLS lower living standard.

- Under the third formula alternative, 50% of the allocation was based on residential energy expenditures and 50% based on heating degree days (not squared) multiplied by the number of households with incomes at or below the BLS lower living standard.

- The fourth option guaranteed states a minimum benefit of $120 for each household that received Aid to Families with Dependent Children (AFDC), SSI, or Food Stamp benefits. The option was added to S. 1724 at the Finance

---

[21] See, for example, Senator Russell Long, "Home Energy Assistance Act," Senate debate, *Congressional Record*, vol. 125, part 25 (November 14, 1979), p. 32278. "But the formula [as passed by the Senate Finance Committee] went a long way toward considering the total household expense for energy, not just heating."

[22] Senator Rudy Boschwitz, "Home Energy Assistance Act," Senate debate, *Congressional Record*, vol. 125, part 25 (November 14, 1979), p. 32290. "I refer back to the committee report, which talks about the intent of the act being to 'offset high heating costs (and cooling where medically necessary) and that assistance not be a supplement of all utilities and their use to run appliances, etc.'... It is very clear that it is the intent of the Senate to help keep people warm."

[23] Senator Edmund Muskie, "Home Energy Assistance Act," Senate debate, *Congressional Record*, vol. 125, part 25 (November 14, 1979), p. 32288. "I do not often do this. As a matter of fact, this is my 21st year in the Senate, and I can recall only one other time in which I have sought to use delay and extended debate to make a point and to achieve justice. I am not a filibusterer. If I did not believe deeply about this, I would not be standing here."

[24] The BLS determined the lower living standard income level through its annual family budgets, which it maintained from 1947 to 1981. At the time the LIEAP program was enacted, the BLS developed annual family budgets assuming three different standards of living: lower, intermediate, and higher. The budget was calculated using costs of consumer goods including food, housing, transportation, clothing, and health care (unlike the federal poverty guidelines, which are based on the amount of money needed to buy food). The budget was then adjusted for family size and the prices of goods in various cities throughout the country. See David S. Johnson, John M. Rogers, and Lucilla Tan, "A Century of Family Budgets in the United States," *Monthly Labor Review*, 124, no. 5 (May 2001): 28-45.

---

Committee level in recognition of the fact that (in general) funds were not being provided for cooling costs.[25]

(See **Table 2** for a breakdown of these formulas.)

While the focus of the formula was on heating assistance, the LIEAP law did allow states to provide for cooling when households could demonstrate medical necessity.[26] Congress authorized LIEAP for one year, FY1981, at $3 billion, but funds were not appropriated as part of P.L. 96-223.

## *Formula Under P.L. 96-369*

Before the formula in P.L. 96-223 could be used to allocate funds, Congress introduced an alternative method for computing the state distribution rates. It did so when it appropriated $1.85 billion in LIEAP funds for FY1981 in a continuing resolution (P.L. 96-369), in October of 1980, six months after enactment of the Crude Oil Windfall Profits Tax Act. The new allocation method was not described in P.L. 96-369, however. Instead, the continuing resolution referred to a House Appropriations Committee report (H. Rept. 96-1244) accompanying another bill—the FY1981 Departments of Labor, Health and Human Services and Education Appropriations Act. It was in this committee report that the additional formula components for LIEAP were laid out.[27] The additional formula components appeared to be intended to act as a counter to the formula developed in P.L. 96-223, which some argued benefitted warmer weather states more than was necessary.[28]

The first step in the new set of formulas was to determine each state's share of funds using two calculations set out in H. Rept. 96-1244 and assign states the greater of the two amounts.

- Under the first formula alternative, 50% of the allocation was based on the increase in home heating expenditures, and 50% was based on the number of heating degree days squared times the population with income less than or equal to 125% of poverty. This was the same formula used for the Low-Income Supplemental Energy Allowances Program.

---

[25] Senator Russell B. Long, "Home Energy Assistance Act," Senate debate, *Congressional Record*, vol. 125, part 25 (November 15, 1979), p. 32561. "This language was evolved in the Finance Committee. When the majority of the committee voted to exclude such items as air-conditioning and anything related to cooling a house and limited that formula to heating, this Senator contended that, if that were to be the case, there should be at least a minimum on which people could depend."

[26] According to the law, "The State is authorized to make grants to eligible households to meet the rising costs of cooling whenever the household establishes that such cooling is the result of medical need pursuant to standards established by the Secretary."

[27] House Committee on Appropriations, report to accompany H.R. 7998, the FY1981 Departments of Labor, Health and Human Services, and Education Appropriations Act, 96th Cong., 2nd sess., H. Rept. 96-1244, August 21, 1980, pp. 75-76.

[28] See, for example, Representative David Obey, "Low Income Energy Assistance," House debate, *Congressional Record*, vol. 126, part 18 (August 27, 1980), p. 23505. "Last year the Congress adopted a formula which, very frankly, was unfair to the South. It provided a much larger amount of the money available than it should have to Northern States. In response to that, Senator Long, on the windfall profit tax legislation, adopted an amendment which, for the block grant portion of the program, provided phenomenal increases for the Southern States at the expense of the Northern States."

---

- Under the second formula alternative, 25% of the allocation was based on total residential energy expenditures, and 75% was based on heating degree days squared multiplied by the number of low-income households in the state.

The greater of the two percentages calculated using the formula in H. Rept. 96-1244 was then assigned to each state. After adjusting state allotments proportionately so that the total allocation reached 100% of funds available, the second step in the amended formula was to compare these state allotments to 75% of the amount each state would receive under the formula in P.L. 96-223. States would then receive the greater of these two amounts. To see the percentage of funds that each state received under the LIEAP formula, see **Table 3**, column (a).

Although the alternative formulas under H.Rept. 96-1244 used factors similar to those in P.L. 96-223, the original set of formulas was somewhat more favorable to warm-weather states. For example, the BLS lower living standard, used in all of the P.L. 96-223 formulas but only one of those in H.Rept. 96-1244, was higher than 125% of poverty for most household sizes, which benefitted the South, where the low-income population was higher.[29] The original set of formulas in P.L. 96-223 also provided for a minimum benefit to states on the basis of the number of AFDC, SSI, and Food Stamp recipient households, unconditioned on their household heating expenditures. In addition, the inclusion of the increase in home heating expenditures in H. Rept. 96-1244 benefitted Northeastern states, where heating oil prices had increased substantially.[30]

### Table 2. Distribution of Funds Under LIEAP

| P.L. 96-223 | P.L. 96-369 |
|---|---|
| Assign each state the option under which they receive the greatest proportion of funds. If Options 2 and 3 both result in a greater proportion than Option 1, assign the state the lesser of Option 2 or 3. | Each state receives the greater of 75% of the amount under P.L. 96-223 or Option 1 or Option 2 under P.L. 96-369. |
| Option 1: ½ Residential energy expenditures | Option 1: ½ Increase in home heating expenditures from 1978-1980[a] |
| ½ (Heating degree days)$^2$ * Households with income ≤ BLS lower living standard | ½ (Heating degree days)$^2$ * Population with income ≤ 125% of poverty |
| Option 2: ¼ Residential energy expenditures | Option 2: ¼ Total residential energy expenditures 1980 |
| ¾ (Heating degree days)$^2$ * Households with income ≤ BLS lower living standard | ¾ (Heating degree days)$^2$ * Households with income ≤ BLS lower living standard |
| Option 3: ½ Residential energy expenditures | |
| ½ Heating degree days * Households with income ≤ BLS lower living standard | |
| Option 4: Funds sufficient for a minimum benefit of $120 per AFDC, SSI, and Food Stamp-recipient household | |

---

[29] "The Low-Income Home Energy Assistance Program: An Analysis of the 1984 Reauthorization Issues," Coalition of Northeastern Governors, April 1984, p. 5.

[30] H.Rept. 96-1244 did not specify the years between which the increase in home heating expenditures should be measured. In implementing the formula, HHS measured the increase between 1978 and 1980.

**Source:** The Crude Oil Windfall Profits Tax Act (P.L. 96-223) and the House Appropriations Committee Report to Accompany H.R. 7998, the FY1981 Departments of Labor, Health and Human Services, and Education Appropriations Bill, H.Rept. 96-1244, August 21, 1980.

**Notes:** * Multiplied by.

≤ Less than or equal to.

a.   H.Rept. 96-1244 did not specify which years would be used to determine residential energy expenditures; 1978 and 1980 were the years used by HHS.

# Enactment of LIHEAP

In August 1981, the Omnibus Budget Reconciliation Act, P.L. 97-35, created LIHEAP, replacing its predecessor, LIEAP. The new program was not substantially different from the previous program. Some of the changes to the program included less restrictive federal rules and more state flexibility in determining how to operate their LIHEAP programs. The program was authorized at $1.85 billion for FY1982-FY1984. In FY1982, Congress appropriated $1.875 billion for LIHEAP; in FY1983, it appropriated $1.975 billion; and in FY1984, $2.075 billion.

## Continued Use of the LIEAP Formula

When the formula for LIEAP was initially created in 1980 under the Crude Oil Windfall Profits Tax Act (P.L. 96-223), it brought about a good deal of debate on the floor of the Senate, where the formula provisions were added to the legislation.[31] Discussion over the formula also occurred leading up to the enactment of P.L. 96-369, the FY1981 continuing resolution that funded LIEAP and amended the formula.[32] Despite these earlier disagreements over formula allocations, the process to enact LIHEAP in 1981 did not engender the same level of debate or result in a different formula. Instead, the law creating LIHEAP provided that the allotment percentages for each state would remain the same as they had been in FY1981 under the LIEAP formula as amended by P.L. 96-369. From FY1982 through FY1984, then, states continued to receive the same percentage of funds that they received under the LIEAP formula.

## The 1984 LIHEAP Reauthorization: A New Formula

### Formula Discussions

When Congress began to consider reauthorizing LIHEAP in 1983, two aspects of the formula were debated. First, some legislators recognized that the multi-step LIEAP formula benefitted cold-weather states relative to warm-weather states.[33] The second debated aspect of the formula centered on the appropriateness and timeliness of the data used in formula calculations. In 1983, the energy information used to calculate state allotments was not the most current data

---

[31] See, for example, Senate debate, *Congressional Record*, vol. 125, parts 24-25 (November 13-15, 1979), pp. 32082-32086, 32275-32293, 32558-32565, and 32576-32589.

[32] House debate, *Congressional Record*, vol. 126, part 18 (August 27, 1980), pp. 23502-23515.

[33] See, for example, Comments of Rep. Billy Tauzin, U.S. Congress, Joint Hearing before the Subcommittees of the Committees on Energy and Commerce, Education and Labor, and Ways and Means, *Energy Costs and Low Income Energy Assistance*, 98th Cong., 1st sess., February 24, 1983, pp. 119-120.

---

available.[34] For example, the most recent data the formula used were the change in the cost of energy between 1978 and 1980, or the cost of energy in 1980, depending on the sub-formula one chose to apply. No aspect of the formula took account of increased costs after 1980.[35]

Legislative sentiment in favor of changing the formula was evident, when, in September 1983, the House adopted an amendment to the Emergency Immigration Education Act (H.R. 3520) that would have adjusted the LIHEAP formula and resulted in a change in allocations to the states. The amendment's formula took into account the energy expenditures of poor families, which, according to the amendment's sponsor, Representative Carlos Moorhead (California), would result in lower percentage allocations for 23 states, mostly in the Northeast and Midwest, gains for 27, primarily in the South, and the same allocation for one state.[36] The amendment was eventually dropped from H.R. 3520 in conference with the Senate.

## Introduction of a Hold-Harmless Level

Efforts to reauthorize LIHEAP began in April 1983 with the introduction of the Low-Income Home Energy Assistance Amendments of 1984 (H.R. 2439). The bill was referred to two committees: Education and Labor and Energy and Commerce. Within the Energy and Commerce committee, two subcommittees held mark-ups: Fossil and Synthetic Fuels and Energy Conservation and Power.

As introduced, H.R. 2439 did not contain changes to the LIHEAP formula. The Subcommittees on Fossil and Synthetic Fuels and Energy Conservation and Power worked together to arrive at a formula change, which had the effect of shifting funds from states in the Northeast to the South and West. Unlike the previous set of formulas developed under LIEAP, the new formula directed the Department of Health and Human Services to determine states' allotments "using data relating to the most recent year for which data is available." Because the cost of heating oil remained steady between 1981 and 1983, and the price of natural gas rose 33%, this meant that states in the Northeast—where heating oil was the primary source of energy—would lose LIHEAP dollars, while states in the South and the Midwest would gain under this provision.[37] In addition, population growth in the South (as well as its higher poverty rates) meant that southern states would benefit from the use of more recent population data.

To offset the losses to certain states resulting from the use of current data, H.R. 2439 also included a hold-harmless provision, or hold-harmless level; this provision ensured that if appropriations were less than or equal to $1.875 billion, states would receive no less than their allotment would have been under the old formula at this appropriations level. The bill additionally increased the LIHEAP authorization level to $2.075 billion for FY1984, $2.26 billion for FY1985, $2.5 billion in FY1986, $2.625 billion for FY1987, and $2.8 billion for FY1988.

---

[34] Report of the Committee on Energy and Commerce to accompany H.R. 2439, the Low-Income Home Energy Assistance Amendments of 1984, 98th Cong., 2nd sess., H.Rept. 98-139, Part 2, May 15, 1984, p. 13.

[35] Ibid., p. 4.

[36] *Congressional Record*, vol. 129, part 17 (September 13, 1983), p. 23877. The greatest increases in percentage allocations were for Florida at 51%, Texas at 44%, and Alabama at 37%. The states whose percentage allocations decreased the most were Vermont at 32%, North Dakota at 24%, and New Hampshire at 23%.

[37] "The Low-Income Home Energy Assistance Program: An Analysis of the 1984 Reauthorization Issues," Coalition of Northeastern Governors, April 1984, p. 9.

## Introduction of a Hold-Harmless Rate

After the House Energy and Commerce Committee reported H.R. 2439 to the House floor—but before the full House could act on the bill—the Senate passed its version of LIHEAP reauthorization as part of the Human Services Reauthorization Act (S. 2565) on October 4, 1984.[38] The Senate bill contained language very similar to H.R. 2439, but made several changes and additions to the formula.

- S. 2565 specified that states' shares of LIHEAP funds would be based on the home energy expenditures of low-income households, not on expenditures of all households.

- The hold-harmless level was altered. S. 2565 directed that no state in FY1985 would receive less funding than it received in FY1984, and for FY1986 and thereafter, no state would receive less than the amount they would have received in FY1984 if the appropriations level had been $1.975 billion.

- A second hold-harmless provision, or hold-harmless rate, was created. The provision maintained the *percentage* allocated rather than a total funding level allocated to each affected state.

The hold-harmless rate provision guaranteed that certain states would receive increased allotments when appropriations reached $2.25 billion. States would qualify for this increase if their total allotment percentage at an appropriation of $2.25 billion were less than 1%. These states would instead receive the allotment rate they would have received at an appropriation of $2.14 billion if that allotment rate were higher than the rate at $2.25 billion. In their debate about S. 2565, Senators referred to the hold-harmless rate as the "small States hold harmless," as the intent was to protect the small (population) states' shares of LIHEAP funds.[39] Otherwise, the concern was that appropriations might have to increase significantly before small state allotments would increase above their hold-harmless levels, with the states' percentage shares of funds declining even as total appropriations increased.

The Senate bill also included different authorization amounts for LIHEAP, $2.14 billion for FY1985 and $2.275 billion for FY1986. After S. 2565 passed the Senate, the House debated and passed the bill on October 9, 1984, retaining all the provisions included in the Senate version. The bill became P.L. 98-558, the Human Services Reauthorization Act, on October 30, 1984.

## LIHEAP Formula Statutory Language

Unlike the allocation formulas under LIEAP and the other energy assistance programs that preceded LIHEAP, which dictated the use of specific variables to determine allotments to the states, the LIHEAP formula as drafted by Congress gives more general guidance to HHS. The LIHEAP statute, as enacted in P.L. 98-558 and codified at 42 U.S.C. Section 8623(a)(2) provides as follows.

---

[38] The final version of S. 2565 can be found in the *Congressional Record*, daily edition, vol. 130 (October 4, 1984), p. S13393.

[39] *Congressional Record*, daily edition, vol. 130 (October 4, 1984), pp. S13415-S13416.

(A) a State's allotment percentage is the percentage which expenditures for home energy by low-income households in that State bears to such expenditures in all States, except that States which thereby receive the greatest proportional increase in allotments by reason of the application of this paragraph from the amount they received pursuant to P.L. 98-139 [the FY1984 appropriation] shall have their allotments reduced to the extent necessary to ensure that—

> (i) no State for fiscal year 1985 shall receive less than the amount of funds the State received in fiscal year 1984; and

> (ii) no State for fiscal year 1986 and thereafter shall receive less than the amount of funds the State would have received in fiscal year 1984 if the appropriations for this subchapter for fiscal year 1984 had been $1,975,000,000, and

(B) any State whose allotment percentage out of funds available to States from a total appropriation of $2,250,000,000 would be less than 1 percent, shall not, in any year when total appropriations equal or exceed $2,250,000,000, have its allotment percentage reduced from the percentage it would receive from a total appropriation of $2,140,000,000.

The next section of this report describes how funds are allocated to the states according to this statutory language.

# Determining LIHEAP Regular Fund Allotments Using the "New" Formula

Current law as enacted in P.L. 98-558, sometimes referred to as the "new" LIHEAP formula, provides for three different methods to calculate each state's allotment of regular LIHEAP funds. The calculation method used to determine state allotments depends upon the size of the appropriation for that fiscal year.

- If the annual appropriation level is at or below the equivalent of a hypothetical FY1984 appropriation of $1.975 billion, then the allocation percentages under the "old" LIHEAP formula apply.

- If appropriations exceed a hypothetical FY1984 appropriation of $1.975 billion, then new formula percentages apply and are used to calculate state allotments. To calculate the new formula percentages, HHS uses the most recent data available to determine the heating and cooling costs of low-income households. When appropriations exceed the $1.975 billion level, but are less than $2.25 billion, the new formula percentages are used together with the hold-harmless level.

- Finally, if appropriations equal or exceed $2.25 billion, the new percentages apply and both the hold-harmless level together with the hold-harmless rate are in effect.

This section describes the steps involved in allocating LIHEAP funds to the states under each of the appropriations triggers.

# Calculating the New Formula Rates

As mentioned previously, when Congress considered a new formula for distributing LIHEAP funds in 1983 and 1984, one of its concerns was the appropriateness and timeliness of the data used in formula calculations. At the time, the energy information used to calculate state allotments under the LIEAP formula did not use the most current data available.[40] In fact, the formula allocations were fixed percentages, and the LIHEAP statute at that time had no provision for allowing newer information to be incorporated into the determination of state allotments. For example, the formula used the change in cost of energy between 1978 and 1980, but did not take account of increased costs after 1980. The LIHEAP formula as created by P.L. 98-558 requires HHS to use the most recent data available. HHS updates these data periodically. The most recent data were provided to CRS in September 2013.

As directed by the statute as enacted in 1984, the LIHEAP formula uses the home energy expenditures of low-income households in each state as a first step in determining the proportion of total regular funds that each state will receive.[41] Specifically, this means estimating the amount of money that all low-income households (as defined by the LIHEAP statute)[42] in each state spend on heating and cooling from all energy sources. This method accounts for variations in heating and cooling needs of the states, the types of energy used, energy prices, and the low-income population and their heating and cooling methods. The process for capturing the expenditures of low-income households for the most current year possible involves the following steps.

- **Total Residential Energy Consumption.** The first step in calculating new formula rates is determining total residential energy consumption for each heating and cooling source in every state. Residential energy consumption is usually measured in terms of the total amount of British Thermal Units (Btus) used in private households and generally captures energy used for space and water heating, cooling, lighting, refrigeration, cooking, and the energy needed to operate appliances. The most recent data used in calculating LIHEAP formula rates come from the 2011 Energy Information Administration (EIA) State Energy Data System consumption estimates.

- **Temperature Variation.** The next step in determining the formula rates involves adjusting the amount of energy consumed for each fuel source by temperature variation in each state. This is done by using a ratio consisting of the 30-year average heating and cooling degree day data to each state's share of the most recent year's average heating and cooling degree days. A heating degree day measures the extent to which a day's average temperature falls below 65°F and a cooling degree day measures the extent to which a day's average temperature rises above 65°F.[43] For example, a day with an average temperature of 50°F results in a measure of 15 heating degree days; a day with an average temperature

---

[40] Report of the Committee on Energy and Commerce to accompany H.R. 2439, the Low-Income Home Energy Amendments of 1984, 98th Cong., 2nd sess., H.Rept. 98-139, Part 2, May 15, 1984, p. 13.

[41] "[A] State's allotment percentage is the percentage which expenditures for home energy by low-income households in that State bears to such expenditures in all States." 42 U.S.C. §8623(a)(2).

[42] The LIHEAP statute considers households with income at or below 150% of poverty or 60% of state median income (whichever value is greater) to be low income. 42 U.S.C. §8624(b)(2)(B).

[43] A state's heating and cooling degree data are weighted by population in the state.

of 80°F results in a measure of 15 cooling degree days. The purpose of the adjustment to fuel consumption is to account for abnormally warm or cool years, where energy usage might attain extreme values. This information is collected by the National Oceanic and Atmospheric Administration. The most recent year's average heating and cooling degree day data are from 2011, and the 30-year average was computed from 1971 to 2000.

- **Heating and Cooling Consumption.** As mentioned above, total residential energy consumption encompasses other uses in addition to heating and cooling (e.g., operation of appliances). So the next step in calculating LIHEAP formula rates is to derive the portion of fuel consumed specifically to heat and cool homes as opposed to other uses. The EIA, as part of the Residential Energy Consumption Survey (RECS), uses an "end use estimation methodology" to estimate the amount of fuel used for heating and cooling (among other uses). The most recent information on heating and cooling consumption comes from the 2005 RECS.[44] HHS adjusts the EIA heating and cooling consumption estimates using heating degree day and cooling degree day data.

- **Low-Income Household Heating and Cooling Consumption.** After estimating heating and cooling consumption for *all* households, the next step is to calculate heating and cooling consumption in Btus for low-income households. HHS uses Census data to determine fuel sources used by low-income households. The most recent information on low-income households and the fuel sources they use comes from the American Community Survey three-year estimates for 2009-2011. In addition, low-income consumption data are adjusted to account for the fact that low-income households might use more or less of a fuel source than is used by households on average. This is done using consumption data from the 2005 RECS.

- **Total Spending on Heating and Cooling.** To arrive at the amount of money that low-income households spend on heating and cooling, the number of Btus used by low-income households that were estimated in the previous step are multiplied by the average fuel price for each fuel source. The total amount spent on heating and cooling by low-income households for each fuel source is then added together to arrive at total spending for each state. Regional energy price variation can be significant, and the formula takes expected expenditure differences into account. This information is collected by the EIA and published in the State Energy Data System Consumption, Price, and Expenditure Estimates.[45] The most recent price data used to calculate formula rates are from 2011.

- **New Formula Percentage.** Finally, these expenditure data are used to estimate the amount spent by low-income households on heating and cooling in each state relative to the amount spent by low-income households on heating and cooling in all states. The calculated proportion becomes the new formula percentage for each state. **Table 3** at the end of this section shows both the percentages under the "old" formula (column (a)) and the most recent "new" formula percentages (column (b)), received by CRS from HHS in September 2013. To see how the formula rates for each state have changed in recent years, see **Table 4**.

---

[44] For more information about the RECS, see the EIA website at http://www.eia.doe.gov/emeu/recs/.

[45] The EIA's state data tables are available at http://www.eia.doe.gov/emeu/states/_seds.html.

These new formula percentages are used to allocate LIHEAP funds to the states if the annual appropriation exceeds the equivalent of a hypothetical FY1984 appropriation of $1.975 billion. However, they do not represent the exact percentage of funds that states will receive under the new formula. The ultimate allotments are determined after application of both the hold-harmless level and hold-harmless rate, described in the next section. The new percentages are the starting point for determining how funds will be allocated to the states.

## Using the New Formula Percentages to Allocate Funds to the States

The LIHEAP new formula percentages that HHS calculates using the most current data available do not necessarily represent the percentage of funds that states will receive. State allotments depend upon the application of the two hold-harmless provisions in the LIHEAP statute. Some states must have their share of funds ratably reduced in order to hold harmless those states that would, but for the hold-harmless provisions, lose funds. Other states see a gain in their share of funds because they benefit from the hold-harmless provisions. The application of the hold-harmless provisions depends upon the size of the appropriation for a given fiscal year. These appropriation level triggers are described below.

### "Old" Formula: Appropriations At or Below $1.975 Billion

The LIHEAP statute does not contain an explicit trigger for the "new" formula rates to be used. However, the statute specifies that states must receive no less than "the amount of funds the State would have received in fiscal year 1984 if the appropriations for this subchapter for fiscal year 1984 had been $1,975,000,000." As a result, up to this appropriation level, states receive the same percentage of funds that they would have received at a given appropriation level under the "old" LIHEAP formula.[46]

The FY1984 appropriation of $1.975 billion referred to in the LIHEAP statute is hypothetical because this was not the amount actually appropriated in FY1984. The actual FY1984 appropriation was $2.075 billion. In addition, the current year appropriation that is "equivalent to" a hypothetical FY1984 appropriation of $1.975 billion is not exactly $1.975 billion. In FY1984, with the exception of funds provided to the territories, all LIHEAP regular funds were distributed to the states. Since then, two other funds have become part of the regular fund distribution. These are funds for training and technical assistance and for the leveraging incentive grants (which includes REACH grants) to the states. This means that an appropriation that is *equivalent to* a hypothetical FY1984 appropriation of $1.975 billion must account for these new funds. Assuming that funds for leveraging incentive/REACH grants would be $27 million and training and technical assistance would be $3 million (amounts that have typically been set aside in the appropriation), then the equivalent of an FY1984 appropriation of $1.975 billion is approximately $2.005 billion.[47]

---

[46] When appropriations are below a hypothetical FY1984 appropriation of $1.975 billion, the result of the current law's hold-harmless provisions is that states receive the same allotment percentages that they did under the old formula. See U.S. Department of Health and Human Services, *Low Income Home Energy Assistance Program: Report to Congress for FY1987*, p. 133.

[47] This amount is arrived at by adding $27 million and $3 million to $1.975 billion.

---

The LIHEAP formula in FY1984 distributed funds by giving states the same percentage of funds that they received in FY1981 under the predecessor program, the Low Income Energy Assistance Program (LIEAP). **Table 3** (later, following the "Implementation of the "New" LIHEAP Formula" section), shows rates under the old formula in column (a). For example, at an appropriation at or below the equivalent of a hypothetical FY1984 appropriation of $1.975 billion, Alabama would receive 0.86% of total funds, Alaska would receive 0.55% of total funds, and so on. **Table A-1**, column (a) reports the dollar amount of funds that each state would have received in FY1984 had the regular fund appropriation been $1.975 billion. For comparison purposes, the dollar amounts also assume that funds for the territories would be 0.5% of the total, a change made by HHS beginning with the FY2014 appropriation.[48]

## "New" Formula with Hold-Harmless Level: Appropriations Between $1.975 Billion and $2.25 Billion

If the regular LIHEAP appropriation exceeds the equivalent of a hypothetical FY1984 appropriation of $1.975 billion for the fiscal year, *all* funds are to be distributed under a different methodology, using the new set of percentages described earlier. In addition, a hold-harmless *level* applies to ensure that certain states do not fall below the amount of funds they would have received at the equivalent of a hypothetical FY1984 appropriation of $1.975 billion.

**Table 3** shows whether a state benefits from the hold-harmless level. This is indicated by a "Y" in column (c), while the dollar amount of funds those states receive by being held harmless appears in column (d). For example, Alabama is not held harmless, while Colorado is held harmless. The dollar amount of funds that Colorado receives pursuant to the hold-harmless level is $31.613 million. But for the hold-harmless level, Colorado would receive less than this dollar amount at its new formula percentage at certain appropriation levels. Eventually, when appropriations increase sufficiently, the percentage of funds under the "new" formula for hold-harmless states will exceed their hold harmless amounts and they will begin to receive their "new" percentage of funds. This appropriation level varies for each state. For example, at lower appropriation levels, the $31.613 million hold-harmless level for Colorado exceeds the state's "new" percentage share of 1.267% of total funds. However, at an appropriation of just over $2.5 billion, Colorado's new percentage share exceeds $31.613 million and the state begins to receive funds at the "new" percentage. Eventually, many states will receive the percentage of funds at their "new" percentage.[49]

The hold-harmless level is achieved by reducing the allocation of funds to states with the greatest proportional gains under the new formula percentages.[50] For example, under the most recent LIHEAP formula percentages, states with the greatest proportional gains were Florida, Arizona, and Texas. Depending on the appropriation level, these states (and others with the greatest gains) may then have their allotments reduced to hold harmless the states that would otherwise see

---

[48] HHS Administration for Children and Families, Office of Community Services, *LIHEAP Dear Colleague Notice Allocation for Territories FY2014*, November 22, 2013, http://www.acf hhs.gov/programs/ocs/resource/liheap-allocation-for-territories-fy-2014.

[49] The exceptions to this are states that benefit from the hold-harmless rate, described in the next section, and the states that are ratably reduced in order to compensate states that benefit from the hold-harmless rate.

[50] "States which thereby receive the greatest proportional increase in allotments ... shall have their allotments reduced to the extent necessary to ensure that ... no State for fiscal year 1986 and thereafter shall receive less than the amount of funds the State would have received in fiscal year 1984." 42 U.S.C. §8623(a)(2)(A)(ii).

reduced benefits. So although these states with the greatest proportional gains will see their LIHEAP allotments increase under the new formula, their allotments may not increase to reach their new formula rates (column (b) of **Table 3**).

Columns (b) and (c) of **Table A-1** show estimated allotments to the states at hypothetical appropriations levels between $1.975 billion and $2.25 billion. Column (b) shows the estimated allotment of funds that each state would receive when the regular fund appropriation is at $2.14 billion and column (c) shows the estimated allotment of funds when the regular fund appropriation is just under $2.25 billion ($2,249,999,999).

## "New" Formula with Hold-Harmless Level and Rate: Appropriations At or Above $2.25 Billion

The LIHEAP statute stipulates additional requirements in the method for distributing funds when the appropriation is at or above $2.25 billion. At this level, the hold-harmless level still applies, but, in addition, a new hold-harmless *rate* is applied. Specifically, for all appropriation levels at or above $2.25 billion, states that would have received less than 1% of a total $2.25 billion appropriation must be allocated the percentage they would have received at a $2.14 billion appropriation level.[51] (This assumes the percentage at $2.14 billion is greater than the percentage originally calculated at the hypothetical $2.25 billion appropriation; this is not true for all states that receive less than 1% of the $2.25 billion appropriation.) Then that state will receive the percentage share of funds it would have received at $2.14 billion for all appropriation levels at or above $2.25 billion. This hold-harmless *rate* ensures a state specific *share* of the total available funds.

As with the hold-harmless level, the allocations to the states with the greatest proportional gains are then ratably reduced again until there is no funding shortfall. Column (e) of **Table 3** shows which states benefit from the hold-harmless rate, indicated by a "Y," while column (f) shows the proportion of funds that those states receive. For example, Idaho benefits from the hold-harmless rate and receives 0.587% of the total appropriation when appropriations are at or above $2.25 billion.

The application of the hold-harmless rate creates another layer of discontinuity in the allocation rates. States that are ratably reduced see their allocations at $2.25 billion fall below the amount they would receive at $2.249 billion, while states that benefit from the hold-harmless rate see their funding jump up slightly. Columns (d) through (h) of **Table A-1** in **Appendix A** show estimated allotments to states at various hypothetical appropriations levels at or above $2.25 billion. Column (d) shows the estimated allotment of funds that each state receives when the regular appropriation is at $2.25 billion after the hold-harmless rate is applied. Columns (e) through (h) show the estimated allotment each state would receive at $2.5 billion, $3.0 billion, $4.0 billion, and $5.1 billion.

---

[51] "[A]ny State whose allotment percentage out of funds available to States from a total appropriation of $2,250,000,000 would be less than 1 percent, shall not, in any year when total appropriations equal or exceed $2,250,000,000, have its allotment percentage reduced from the percentage it would receive from a total appropriation of $2,140,000,000." 42 U.S.C. §8623(a)(2)(B).

# Implementation of the "New" LIHEAP Formula

Until FY2006, appropriations for regular LIHEAP funds had only exceeded the equivalent of a hypothetical FY1984 appropriation of $1.975 billion in 1985 and 1986; thereafter, from FY1987 through FY2005, and again in FY2007, states continued to receive the same percentage of LIHEAP funds that they received under the program's predecessor, LIEAP (see column (a) of **Table 3** for these percentages). In FY2006, funds were distributed under the "new" LIHEAP formula when Congress appropriated $2.48 billion in regular funds for the program. In FY2008, perhaps due to an oversight, the new formula was again used to distribute funds. The FY2008 Consolidated Appropriations Act (P.L. 110-161) failed to authorize a set-aside called leveraging incentive grants. As a result, the funds for those grants were added to the LIHEAP regular funds, triggering the new formula.[52] In FY2009, the Consolidated Security, Disaster Assistance, and Continuing Appropriations Act (P.L. 110-329) appropriated $4.51 billion in regular funds. However, the law further specified that $840 million be distributed according to the "new" LIHEAP formula, with the remaining $3.67 billion distributed according to the percentages of the "old" formula established by LIEAP. From FY2010 to FY2014, Congress has continued to appropriate funds using a version of a split between the "old" and "new" formulas. See **Table C-1** in **Appendix C** of this report for the distribution of funds to the states from FY2008 through FY2014.

**Table 3. Low-Income Home Energy Program (LIHEAP):**
**"Old" and "New" Allotment Percentages by State, FY2014**

| State | "Old" Allotment Percentage (%) (a) | "New" Allotment Percentage (%) (b) | Hold-Harmless Level[a] | | Hold-Harmless Rate | |
|---|---|---|---|---|---|---|
| | | | State Held Harmless? (c) | Hold-Harmless Level ($Millions) (d) | State Held Harmless? (e) | Hold-Harmless Rate (%) (f) |
| Alabama | 0.860 | 1.686 | N | — | N | — |
| Alaska | 0.549 | 0.563 | N | — | N | — |
| Arizona | 0.416 | 1.379 | N | — | N | — |
| Arkansas | 0.656 | 0.876 | N | — | N | — |
| California | 4.614 | 4.536 | Y | 90.669 | N | — |
| Colorado | 1.609 | 1.270 | Y | 31.613 | N | — |
| Connecticut | 2.099 | 2.371 | N | — | N | — |
| Delaware | 0.279 | 0.427 | N | — | N | — |
| District of Columbia | 0.326 | 0.149 | Y | 6.405 | Y | 0.305 |
| Florida | 1.361 | 5.201 | N | — | N | — |
| Georgia | 1.076 | 3.166 | N | — | N | — |
| Hawaii | 0.108 | 0.230 | N | — | N | — |
| Idaho | 0.628 | 0.371 | Y | 12.331 | Y | 0.587 |

[52] For more information about this issue, see **Appendix C** of this report.

| State | "Old" Allotment Percentage (%) (a) | "New" Allotment Percentage (%) (b) | Hold-Harmless Level[a] State Held Harmless? (c) | Hold-Harmless Level ($Millions) (d) | Hold-Harmless Rate State Held Harmless? (e) | Hold-Harmless Rate (%) (f) |
|---|---|---|---|---|---|---|
| Illinois | 5.809 | 4.510 | Y | 114.147 | N | — |
| Indiana | 2.630 | 1.934 | Y | 51.683 | N | — |
| Iowa | 1.864 | 1.065 | Y | 36.628 | N | — |
| Kansas | 0.856 | 0.945 | N | — | N | — |
| Kentucky | 1.369 | 1.457 | N | — | N | — |
| Louisiana | 0.879 | 1.387 | N | — | N | — |
| Maine | 1.360 | 1.041 | Y | 26.717 | N | — |
| Maryland | 1.607 | 2.193 | N | — | N | — |
| Massachusetts | 4.198 | 4.138 | Y | 82.495 | N | — |
| Michigan | 5.515 | 4.681 | Y | 108.373 | N | — |
| Minnesota | 3.973 | 1.921 | Y | 78.076 | N | — |
| Mississippi | 0.737 | 0.953 | N | — | N | — |
| Missouri | 2.320 | 2.021 | Y | 45.595 | N | — |
| Montana | 0.736 | 0.314 | Y | 14.464 | Y | 0.689 |
| Nebraska | 0.922 | 0.561 | Y | 18.114 | Y | 0.863 |
| Nevada | 0.195 | 0.537 | N | — | N | — |
| New Hampshire | 0.795 | 0.731 | Y | 15.615 | Y | 0.744 |
| New Jersey | 3.897 | 3.620 | Y | 76.584 | N | — |
| New Mexico | 0.521 | 0.394 | Y | 10.233 | Y | 0.487 |
| New York | 12.725 | 9.318 | Y | 250.058 | N | — |
| North Carolina | 1.896 | 2.891 | N | — | N | — |
| North Dakota | 0.800 | 0.254 | Y | 15.712 | Y | 0.748 |
| Ohio | 5.139 | 4.368 | Y | 100.980 | N | — |
| Oklahoma | 0.791 | 1.219 | N | — | N | — |
| Oregon | 1.247 | 0.781 | Y | 24.502 | N | — |
| Pennsylvania | 6.835 | 5.720 | Y | 134.318 | N | — |
| Rhode Island | 0.691 | 0.712 | N | — | N | — |
| South Carolina | 0.683 | 1.403 | N | — | N | — |
| South Dakota | 0.649 | 0.240 | Y | 12.761 | Y | 0.608 |
| Tennessee | 1.386 | 1.848 | N | — | N | — |
| Texas | 2.264 | 6.942 | N | — | N | — |

| State | "Old" Allotment Percentage (%) (a) | "New" Allotment Percentage (%) (b) | Hold-Harmless Level[a] | | Hold-Harmless Rate | |
|---|---|---|---|---|---|---|
| | | | State Held Harmless? (c) | Hold-Harmless Level ($Millions) (d) | State Held Harmless? (e) | Hold-Harmless Rate (%) (f) |
| Utah | 0.748 | 0.494 | Y | 14.691 | Y | 0.700 |
| Vermont | 0.596 | 0.425 | Y | 11.704 | Y | 0.557 |
| Virginia | 1.957 | 2.607 | N | — | N | — |
| Washington | 2.051 | 1.305 | Y | 40.302 | N | — |
| West Virginia | 0.906 | 0.631 | Y | 17.799 | Y | 0.848 |
| Wisconsin | 3.576 | 2.054 | Y | 70.280 | N | — |
| Wyoming | 0.299 | 0.160 | Y | 5.882 | Y | 0.280 |

**Source:** New allotment percentages were provided to CRS by HHS in September 2013. Information in columns (c) through (f) are based on CRS calculations using the new allotment percentages. The calculations assume that funding would be provided for leveraging incentive/REACH grants, training and technical assistance, and 0.5% for the territories.

**Notes:** The actual percentage of total regular funds each state receives at funding levels above $1.975 billion may differ from the new formula percentages due to the hold-harmless provisions and the ratable reductions of some states to cover shortfall from these hold-harmless provisions.

a.  The states that benefit from the hold-harmless level vary depending on the amount appropriated for LIHEAP regular funds. The states listed here benefit from the hold-harmless level when appropriations just exceed the equivalent of an FY1984 appropriation of $1.975 billion.

## Table 4. Recent State Allotment Percentages Under the "New" LIHEAP Formula

(Fiscal years indicate when new formula rates would have been used to distribute funds to states)

| States | "Old" Formula Percentages | "New" Formula Percentages | | | | | | |
|---|---|---|---|---|---|---|---|---|
| | | FY2008 | FY2009 | FY2010 | FY2011 | FY2012 | FY2013 | FY2014 |
| Alabama | 0.860% | 1.932% | 1.650% | 1.582% | 1.599% | 1.583% | 1.716% | 1.686% |
| Alaska | 0.549 | 0.376 | 0.317 | 0.575 | 0.511 | 0.398 | 0.522 | 0.563 |
| Arizona | 0.416 | 0.992 | 0.813 | 1.018 | 1.098 | 1.132 | 1.326 | 1.379 |
| Arkansas | 0.656 | 1.082 | 0.910 | 0.884 | 0.852 | 0.899 | 0.876 | 0.876 |
| California | 4.614 | 5.690 | 5.303 | 4.479 | 4.453 | 4.452 | 4.433 | 4.536 |
| Colorado | 1.609 | 1.280 | 1.305 | 1.333 | 1.247 | 1.267 | 1.264 | 1.270 |
| Connecticut | 2.099 | 1.732 | 2.164 | 2.205 | 2.239 | 2.398 | 2.416 | 2.371 |
| Delaware | 0.279 | 0.435 | 0.453 | 0.375 | 0.373 | 0.375 | 0.421 | 0.427 |
| District of Columbia | 0.326 | 0.309 | 0.328 | 0.181 | 0.192 | 0.194 | 0.184 | 0.149 |
| Florida | 1.361 | 4.187 | 3.781 | 4.728 | 4.583 | 4.593 | 5.475 | 5.201 |
| Georgia | 1.076 | 2.829 | 2.734 | 2.620 | 2.641 | 2.742 | 3.137 | 3.166 |
| Hawaii | 0.108 | 0.101 | 0.099 | 0.150 | 0.150 | 0.205 | 0.185 | 0.230 |
| Idaho | 0.628 | 0.386 | 0.331 | 0.396 | 0.349 | 0.335 | 0.339 | 0.371 |

| States | "Old" Formula Percentages | "New" Formula Percentages | | | | | | |
|---|---|---|---|---|---|---|---|---|
| | | FY2008 | FY2009 | FY2010 | FY2011 | FY2012 | FY2013 | FY2014 |
| Illinois | 5.809 | 4.796 | 4.998 | 4.843 | 5.014 | 5.243 | 4.655 | 4.510 |
| Indiana | 2.630 | 2.209 | 2.128 | 2.147 | 2.080 | 2.209 | 1.814 | 1.934 |
| Iowa | 1.864 | 1.085 | 1.064 | 1.028 | 1.099 | 1.080 | 1.001 | 1.065 |
| Kansas | 0.856 | 1.105 | 1.106 | 0.978 | 0.993 | 0.967 | 1.002 | 0.945 |
| Kentucky | 1.369 | 1.688 | 1.621 | 1.243 | 1.256 | 1.344 | 1.329 | 1.457 |
| Louisiana | 0.879 | 1.704 | 1.514 | 1.324 | 1.365 | 1.414 | 1.378 | 1.387 |
| Maine | 1.360 | 0.722 | 0.908 | 1.127 | 1.090 | 1.010 | 0.927 | 1.041 |
| Maryland | 1.607 | 2.421 | 2.652 | 1.965 | 2.080 | 2.197 | 2.344 | 2.193 |
| Massachusetts | 4.198 | 3.043 | 3.311 | 3.757 | 3.718 | 3.730 | 4.032 | 4.138 |
| Michigan | 5.515 | 4.651 | 4.645 | 5.040 | 4.819 | 4.863 | 4.966 | 4.681 |
| Minnesota | 3.973 | 1.789 | 1.917 | 2.023 | 2.025 | 2.047 | 1.849 | 1.921 |
| Mississippi | 0.737 | 1.105 | 0.951 | 0.974 | 0.940 | 0.990 | 0.955 | 0.953 |
| Missouri | 2.320 | 2.497 | 2.309 | 2.014 | 2.011 | 1.829 | 1.963 | 2.021 |
| Montana | 0.736 | 0.414 | 0.441 | 0.295 | 0.287 | 0.328 | 0.280 | 0.314 |
| Nebraska | 0.922 | 0.598 | 0.558 | 0.547 | 0.553 | 0.591 | 0.555 | 0.561 |
| Nevada | 0.195 | 0.686 | 0.576 | 0.500 | 0.526 | 0.498 | 0.563 | 0.537 |
| New Hampshire | 0.795 | 0.453 | 0.503 | 0.612 | 0.605 | 0.742 | 0.623 | 0.731 |
| New Jersey | 3.897 | 2.838 | 3.621 | 3.995 | 4.105 | 4.010 | 3.812 | 3.620 |
| New Mexico | 0.521 | 0.628 | 0.577 | 0.458 | 0.441 | 0.430 | 0.407 | 0.394 |
| New York | 12.725 | 8.491 | 9.393 | 9.520 | 10.018 | 10.227 | 9.445 | 9.318 |
| North Carolina | 1.896 | 3.186 | 3.261 | 2.766 | 2.823 | 2.619 | 2.954 | 2.891 |
| North Dakota | 0.800 | 0.235 | 0.273 | 0.246 | 0.256 | 0.302 | 0.215 | 0.254 |
| Ohio | 5.139 | 4.512 | 4.803 | 4.893 | 4.941 | 4.687 | 4.243 | 4.368 |
| Oklahoma | 0.791 | 1.452 | 1.275 | 1.236 | 1.224 | 1.152 | 1.207 | 1.219 |
| Oregon | 1.247 | 1.008 | 0.750 | 0.715 | 0.702 | 0.664 | 0.712 | 0.781 |
| Pennsylvania | 6.835 | 5.174 | 5.731 | 5.993 | 5.885 | 5.807 | 5.571 | 5.720 |
| Rhode Island | 0.691 | 0.596 | 0.665 | 0.635 | 0.615 | 0.670 | 0.753 | 0.712 |
| South Carolina | 0.683 | 1.425 | 1.349 | 1.278 | 1.260 | 1.201 | 1.394 | 1.403 |
| South Dakota | 0.649 | 0.268 | 0.235 | 0.249 | 0.253 | 0.272 | 0.233 | 0.240 |
| Tennessee | 1.386 | 2.055 | 1.801 | 1.743 | 1.717 | 1.700 | 1.865 | 1.848 |
| Texas | 2.264 | 7.095 | 6.524 | 7.668 | 7.349 | 7.135 | 7.183 | 6.942 |
| Utah | 0.748 | 0.648 | 0.599 | 0.559 | 0.508 | 0.413 | 0.452 | 0.494 |
| Vermont | 0.596 | 0.356 | 0.319 | 0.418 | 0.419 | 0.396 | 0.417 | 0.425 |
| Virginia | 1.957 | 2.817 | 3.041 | 2.428 | 2.486 | 2.490 | 2.581 | 2.607 |

| States | "Old" Formula Percentages | "New" Formula Percentages | | | | | | |
|---|---|---|---|---|---|---|---|---|
| | | FY2008 | FY2009 | FY2010 | FY2011 | FY2012 | FY2013 | FY2014 |
| Washington | 2.051 | 1.621 | 1.204 | 1.225 | 1.245 | 1.145 | 1.244 | 1.305 |
| West Virginia | 0.906 | 0.960 | 0.907 | 0.663 | 0.639 | 0.638 | 0.625 | 0.631 |
| Wisconsin | 3.576 | 2.108 | 2.080 | 2.229 | 2.236 | 2.230 | 2.010 | 2.054 |
| Wyoming | 0.299 | 0.233 | 0.202 | 0.137 | 0.129 | 0.154 | 0.146 | 0.160 |

**Source:** State data were received by CRS from HHS in December 2005, May 2007, September 2008, April 2009, June 2010, August 2011, August 2012, and September 2013.

# Appendix A. Estimated Allotments to the States Under Various Hypothetical Appropriations Levels

**Table A-1**, below, shows estimated allocations to the states at various hypothetical appropriations levels. In column (a) are allotments at the equivalent of a hypothetical FY1984 appropriation of $1.975 billion—under current LIHEAP practice where funds are set aside for leveraging incentive grants and training and technical assistance, the equivalent appropriation level is approximately $2.005 billion. The remaining columns show estimated allotments at appropriations of $2.14 billion, just under $2.25 billion, $2.25 billion, $3.0 billion, $4.0 billion, and $5.1 billion, the amount at which the LIHEAP program was last authorized in P.L. 109-58. In each case, the estimates assume that 0.5% would be set aside for the territories, the amount set aside by HHS in FY2014.

## Table A-1. LIHEAP Estimated State Allotments for Regular Funds at Various Hypothetical Appropriation Levels

($ in millions)

| State | "Old" Formula Hypothetical $1.975 Billion in FY1984 (a) | "New" Formula, Hold-Harmless Level Only $2.14 Billion (b) | Just Under $2.25 Billion (c) | $2.25 Billion (d) | "New" Formula, Hold-Harmless Level and Rate $2.5 Billion (e) | $3.0 Billion (f) | $4.0 Billion (g) | $5.1 Billion (h) |
|---|---|---|---|---|---|---|---|---|
| Alabama | 16.901 | 22.303 | 27.610 | 27.007 | 41.255 | 49.822 | 66.597 | 85.049 |
| Alaska | 10.788 | 11.816 | 12.432 | 12.432 | 13.832 | 16.632 | 22.232 | 28.391 |
| Arizona | 8.174 | 10.786 | 13.353 | 13.061 | 19.951 | 30.557 | 44.777 | 57.402 |
| Arkansas | 12.896 | 17.019 | 19.355 | 19.355 | 21.535 | 25.894 | 34.613 | 44.203 |
| California | 90.669 | 95.224 | 100.188 | 100.188 | 111.471 | 134.036 | 179.166 | 228.808 |
| Colorado | 31.613 | 31.613 | 31.613 | 31.613 | 31.613 | 37.542 | 50.183 | 64.087 |
| Connecticut | 41.241 | 49.788 | 52.383 | 52.383 | 58.282 | 70.080 | 93.676 | 119.632 |
| Delaware | 5.474 | 7.224 | 8.942 | 8.747 | 10.487 | 12.610 | 16.856 | 21.527 |
| District of Columbia | 6.405 | 6.405 | 6.405 | 6.739 | 7.498 | 9.015 | 12.051 | 15.390 |
| Florida | 26.742 | 35.291 | 43.687 | 42.732 | 65.277 | 99.977 | 146.502 | 187.809 |
| Georgia | 21.144 | 27.903 | 34.542 | 33.787 | 51.612 | 79.047 | 115.832 | 148.492 |
| Hawaii | 2.129 | 2.810 | 3.479 | 3.402 | 5.198 | 6.790 | 9.077 | 11.592 |
| Idaho | 12.331 | 12.331 | 12.331 | 12.974 | 14.435 | 17.357 | 23.202 | 29.630 |
| Illinois | 114.147 | 114.147 | 114.147 | 114.147 | 114.147 | 133.279 | 178.154 | 227.516 |
| Indiana | 51.683 | 51.683 | 51.683 | 51.683 | 51.683 | 57.139 | 76.378 | 97.540 |
| Iowa | 36.628 | 36.628 | 36.628 | 36.628 | 36.628 | 36.628 | 42.070 | 53.727 |
| Kansas | 16.821 | 19.831 | 20.864 | 20.864 | 23.214 | 27.913 | 37.312 | 47.650 |

| State | "Old" Formula Hypothetical $1.975 Billion in FY1984 (a) | "New" Formula, Hold-Harmless Level Only | | "New" Formula, Hold-Harmless Level and Rate | | | | |
|---|---|---|---|---|---|---|---|---|
| | | $2.14 Billion (b) | Just Under $2.25 Billion (c) | $2.25 Billion (d) | $2.5 Billion (e) | $3.0 Billion (f) | $4.0 Billion (g) | $5.1 Billion (h) |
| Kentucky | 26.895 | 30.586 | 32.180 | 32.180 | 35.804 | 43.052 | 57.547 | 73.492 |
| Louisiana | 17.279 | 22.802 | 28.227 | 27.610 | 34.083 | 40.983 | 54.782 | 69.960 |
| Maine | 26.717 | 26.717 | 26.717 | 26.717 | 26.717 | 30.776 | 41.139 | 52.537 |
| Maryland | 31.578 | 41.671 | 48.445 | 48.445 | 53.900 | 64.811 | 86.633 | 110.637 |
| Massachusetts | 82.495 | 86.870 | 91.399 | 91.399 | 101.692 | 122.277 | 163.448 | 208.735 |
| Michigan | 108.373 | 108.373 | 108.373 | 108.373 | 115.030 | 138.316 | 184.887 | 236.115 |
| Minnesota | 78.076 | 78.076 | 78.076 | 78.076 | 78.076 | 78.076 | 78.076 | 96.919 |
| Mississippi | 14.490 | 19.122 | 21.040 | 21.040 | 23.410 | 28.149 | 37.626 | 48.051 |
| Missouri | 45.595 | 45.595 | 45.595 | 45.595 | 49.677 | 59.733 | 79.845 | 101.969 |
| Montana | 14.464 | 14.464 | 14.464 | 15.218 | 16.932 | 20.359 | 27.214 | 34.754 |
| Nebraska | 18.114 | 18.114 | 18.114 | 19.058 | 21.205 | 25.497 | 34.082 | 43.525 |
| Nevada | 3.839 | 5.066 | 6.271 | 6.134 | 9.371 | 14.352 | 21.030 | 26.960 |
| New Hampshire | 15.615 | 15.615 | 16.147 | 16.429 | 18.279 | 21.979 | 29.379 | 37.520 |
| New Jersey | 76.584 | 76.584 | 79.967 | 79.967 | 88.973 | 106.983 | 143.004 | 182.628 |
| New Mexico | 10.233 | 10.233 | 10.233 | 10.766 | 11.979 | 14.403 | 19.253 | 24.587 |
| New York | 250.058 | 250.058 | 250.058 | 250.058 | 250.058 | 275.358 | 368.071 | 470.055 |
| North Carolina | 37.266 | 49.178 | 60.880 | 59.549 | 71.053 | 85.436 | 114.202 | 145.845 |
| North Dakota | 15.712 | 15.712 | 15.712 | 16.531 | 18.393 | 22.116 | 29.563 | 37.754 |
| Ohio | 100.980 | 100.980 | 100.980 | 100.980 | 107.340 | 129.068 | 172.526 | 220.329 |

| State | "Old" Formula Hypothetical $1.975 Billion in FY1984 (a) | "New" Formula, Hold-Harmless Level Only | | "New" Formula, Hold-Harmless Level and Rate | | | | |
|---|---|---|---|---|---|---|---|---|
| | | $2.14 Billion (b) | Just Under $2.25 Billion (c) | $2.25 Billion (d) | $2.5 Billion (e) | $3.0 Billion (f) | $4.0 Billion (g) | $5.1 Billion (h) |
| Oklahoma | 15.535 | 20.501 | 25.379 | 24.825 | 29.970 | 36.037 | 48.171 | 61.518 |
| Oregon | 24.502 | 24.502 | 24.502 | 24.502 | 24.502 | 24.502 | 30.846 | 39.393 |
| Pennsylvania | 134.318 | 134.318 | 134.318 | 134.318 | 140.581 | 169.039 | 225.954 | 288.561 |
| Rhode Island | 13.579 | 14.956 | 15.736 | 15.736 | 17.508 | 21.052 | 28.140 | 35.937 |
| South Carolina | 13.423 | 17.713 | 21.928 | 21.449 | 32.765 | 41.458 | 55.417 | 70.772 |
| South Dakota | 12.761 | 12.761 | 12.761 | 13.426 | 14.938 | 17.962 | 24.010 | 30.663 |
| Tennessee | 27.245 | 35.953 | 40.830 | 40.830 | 45.428 | 54.623 | 73.015 | 93.246 |
| Texas | 44.490 | 58.712 | 72.681 | 71.092 | 108.600 | 166.328 | 243.730 | 312.452 |
| Utah | 14.691 | 14.691 | 14.691 | 15.457 | 17.197 | 20.679 | 27.641 | 35.300 |
| Vermont | 11.704 | 11.704 | 11.704 | 12.314 | 13.701 | 16.474 | 22.021 | 28.122 |
| Virginia | 38.465 | 50.760 | 57.586 | 57.586 | 64.071 | 77.041 | 102.980 | 131.514 |
| Washington | 40.302 | 40.302 | 40.302 | 40.302 | 40.302 | 40.302 | 51.552 | 65.836 |
| West Virginia | 17.799 | 17.799 | 17.799 | 18.727 | 20.836 | 25.053 | 33.489 | 42.768 |
| Wisconsin | 70.280 | 70.280 | 70.280 | 70.280 | 70.280 | 70.280 | 81.137 | 103.618 |
| Wyoming | 5.882 | 5.882 | 5.882 | 6.189 | 6.885 | 8.279 | 11.067 | 14.133 |
| Total | 1,965.125 | 2,099.450 | 2,208.900 | 2,208.900 | 2,457.650 | 2,955.150 | 3,950.150 | 5,044.650 |

**Source:** Congressional Research Service (CRS) calculations based on factors provided by the Department of Health and Human Services (HHS) in September 2013.

**Notes:** These estimates take into account current law, which allows HHS to set aside funds out of regular LIHEAP funds for territories, leverage incentive grants and Residential Energy Assistance Challenge (REACH) grants and training and technical assistance. For each estimate, 0.5% is allocated to the territories, $27 million to leveraging incentive and REACH grants, and $3 million to training and technical assistance. Differing allocations for these purposes could change state allotments.

# Appendix B. Further Depiction of How State Allotments Depend Upon Appropriation Levels

**Figure B-1** graphically illustrates state allotments for three "typical" types of states over a range of appropriations from $0 to $5.1 billion. Represented are (1) a hold-harmless level state, (2) a hold-harmless level and rate state, and (3) a state whose increased allocations are ratably reduced in order to maintain allocations for the hold-harmless level and rate states.

In the figure, there are three vertical areas. These areas separate the three levels of appropriations that are triggers under current law and were explained previously in this report. The figure also graphs the three basic types of states. Reading from top to bottom of **Figure B-1**, these three types of states are as follows.

- **Hold-Harmless Level Only States.** These states are subject to only the hold-harmless level provision. They do not qualify for the hold-harmless rate because each state's share of the regular funds at $2.25 billion is greater than 1%. An example of a hold-harmless level only state is represented by the line that runs from $0 to point G. The hold-harmless level is evident from point A to point F. Here, despite increases in the appropriations level, the state allotment remains fixed. *In Table 3, these are the states that have a "Y" in column (c) and an "N" in column (e).*

- **Ratable Reduction States.** These states are subject to a ratable reduction. Their new formula percentage is greater than their old (FY1984) percentage. An example of these states is depicted by the line that runs from $0 to point H. There is a small decrease in state allotments at point D that is attributable to the increased shortfall on the distribution of funds that the hold-harmless *rate* imposes. *In Table 3, these are the states that have an "N" in both column (c) and column (e).*

- **Hold-Harmless Level *and* Rate States.** These states are subject to both the hold-harmless level and the hold harmless rate provisions. An example of a typical level and rate state is shown by the line that runs from $0 to point I. The hold-harmless level is evident by the fixed state allotment from point C to point E. However, the (subtle) jump at exactly $2.25 billion signals that this state is subject to the hold-harmless *rate* provision. After the allotment jump at $2.25 billion, the state's allotment continues to increase (at a rate lower than the old rate, but higher than the new rate). *In Table 3, these are the states that have a "Y" in column (c) and a "Y" in the column (e).*

# Figure B-1. Estimated LIHEAP Allocations at Various Hypothetical Appropriations Levels for Three Types of States

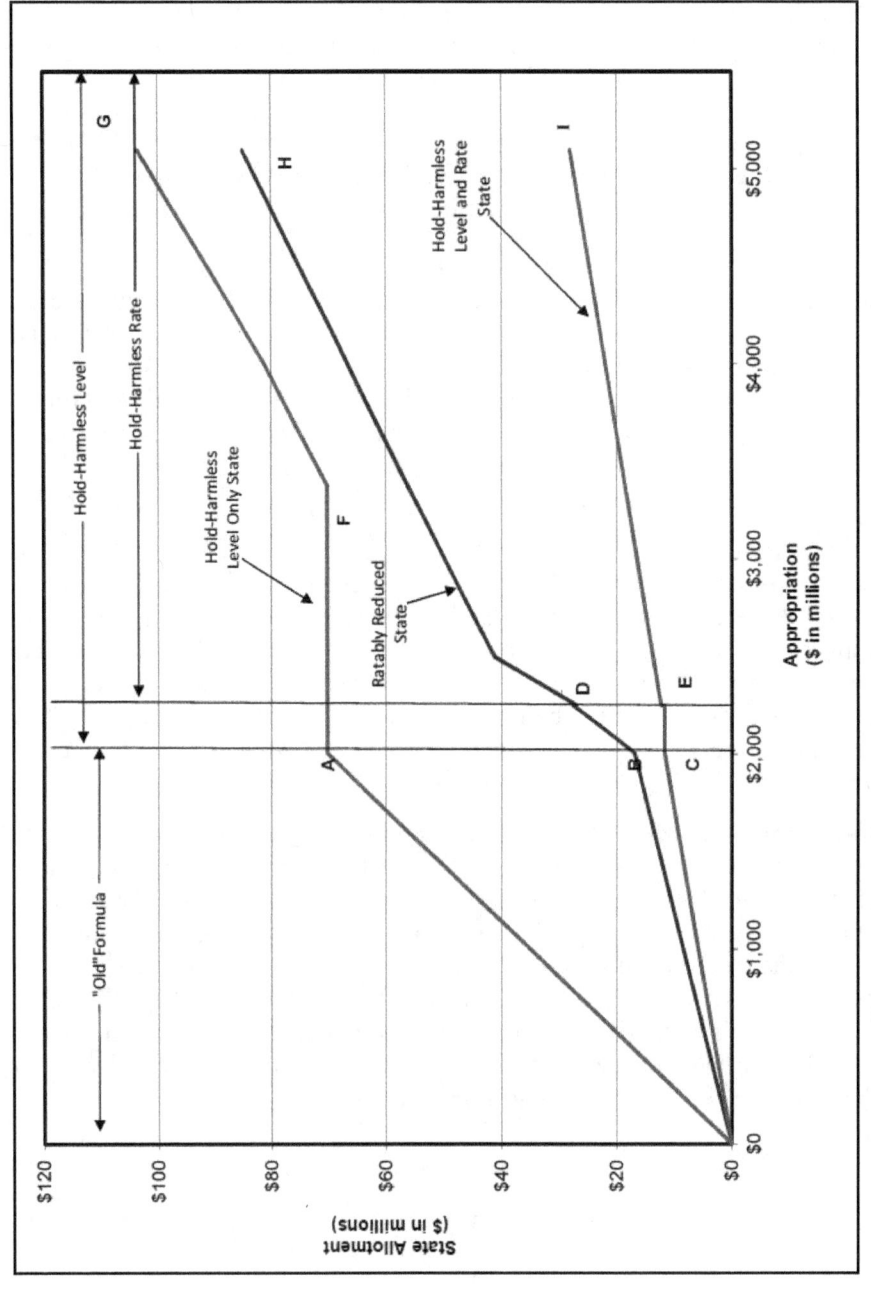

**Source:** Figure created by CRS using formula rates provided by HHS in September 2013.

# Appendix C. LIHEAP Regular Fund Allocations to the States, FY2008-FY2014, and Estimated FY2015 Allocations

**Table C-1**, below, shows actual LIHEAP regular fund allocations to the states from FY2008 through FY2014 and estimated allocations for FY2015 based on the President's budget request.

For FY2015, the President's budget proposed a total of $2.550 billion for LIHEAP regular funds. Of that amount, $366 million would be distributed according to the "new" LIHEAP formula, with the remainder, about $2.184 billion, distributed according to the "old" formula percentages. The budget request would set aside $3 million for training and technical assistance and $27 million for leveraging incentive and REACH grants. Column (h) of **Table C-1** shows estimated allocations to the states based on the President's budget.

Congress appropriated approximately $3.425 billion for LIHEAP as part of the Consolidated Appropriation Act (P.L. 113-76). Prior to distribution of funds, HHS reduced the amount available by 1%, transferring $34.245 billion within the agency. Of the $3.390 billion available, HHS increased the amount available for the territories to 0.5% of the total; this was the first time since the program's inception that the territorial allocation changed from 0.134%. Of the amount available to the states and tribes, $491 million was distributed according to the "new" formula and the remainder according to the "old" formula. See column (g) of **Table C-1**.

Column (f) of **Table C-1** contains actual regular fund allocations to the states in FY2013. The amount appropriated for LIHEAP as part of the FY2013 Consolidated and Further Continuing Appropriations Act (P.L. 113-6) was the same as the FY2012 level—$3.472 billion for regular funds, with $497 million distributed according to the "new" LIHEAP formula. However, application of an across-the-board rescission of 0.2%, sequestration, and a transfer of funds within HHS reduced the total amount available to $3.255 billion.

Column (e) contains actual allocations for FY2012 at an appropriations level of $3.472 billion (P.L. 112-74). The law provided a total of $3.478 billion for LIHEAP regular funds, but the amount was reduced by an across-the-board rescission of 0.189% for discretionary accounts, resulting in the $3.472 billion funding level. P.L. 112-74 also provided that, of the amount appropriated, all but $497 million be distributed according to the proportions of the "old" LIHEAP formula. In addition, $3 million was set aside for training and technical assistance.

In FY2009 (P.L. 110-329), FY2010 (P.L. 111-117), and FY2011 (P.L. 112-10) Congress appropriated $4.51 billion for LIHEAP formula funds. Of this amount, $840 million was distributed according to the "new" LIHEAP formula and the remaining funds, approximately $3.67 billion, according to the "old" formula. Column (d) of **Table C-1** shows the allocations to the states in FY2011, column (c) shows allocations to the states in FY2010, and column (b) shows FY2009 allocations. Note that funds were not distributed in exactly the same way in each year for several reasons. LIHEAP formula rates are updated each year, which affects the percentage of funds that states receive. In addition, two factors changed the FY2011 appropriation. The appropriations bill subjected all discretionary accounts to an across-the-board rescission of 0.2%, and HHS did not distribute leveraging incentive and REACH grants, making the total available to the states slightly more than in FY2009 and FY2010.

In the FY2008 Consolidated Appropriations Act (P.L. 110-161), Congress appropriated $1.98 billion in LIHEAP regular funds.[53] The first distribution to the states of the regular funds appropriated in P.L. 110-161 occurred in December 2007; allocations were made on the basis of the proportions of the "old" LIHEAP formula. Then, on June 26, 2008, HHS announced that it would distribute funds that were thought to have been allocated to leveraging incentive and REACH grants in the FY2008 Appropriations Act as part of the regular fund formula grants. Since the early 1990s, leveraging incentive and REACH grants have been made to states and tribes on the basis of their ability to obtain non-LIHEAP resources for energy assistance (leveraging incentive grants) and for increasing energy efficiency of low-income households (REACH grants). In recent years, Congress has allocated about $27 million for these two funds. However, in FY2008, P.L. 110-161 did not appropriate funds for leveraging incentive and REACH grants. When HHS discovered that language to appropriate the funds was missing from the law, it released the $26.7 million that would otherwise have been distributed as leveraging incentive and REACH grants as part of the LIHEAP formula distribution. The addition of nearly $27 million to the formula grants caused the funds to be released under the "new" LIHEAP formula. Column (a) of **Table C-1** shows the total amount of funds that each state received after $26.7 million was added and funds were distributed under the new formula.

---

[53] P.L. 110-161 contained an across-the-board rescission of 1.747% that reduced the stated amounts appropriated for most Departments of Labor, Health and Human Services, and Education programs. See Division G, §528 of P.L. 110-161. The $1.98 billion appropriation for regular funds was the amount available after this rescission.

## Table C-1. LIHEAP Actual State Regular Fund Allocations for FY2008 through FY2014 and Estimated Allocations for FY2015

($ in millions)

| State | FY2008 Allocations: $1.98 Billion[a] (a) | FY2009 Allocations: $4.51 Billion[b] (b) | FY2010 Allocations: $4.51 Billion[c] (c) | FY2011 Allocations: $4.50 Billion[d] (d) | FY2012 Allocations: $3.47 Billion[e] (e) | FY2013 Allocations: $3.26 Billion[f] (f) | FY2014 Allocations: $3.39 Billion[g] (g) | FY2015 Estimated Allocations FY2015 President's Budget Request: $2.55 Billion[h] (h) |
|---|---|---|---|---|---|---|---|---|
| Alabama | 17.111 | 60.063 | 58.799 | 59.419 | 47.408 | 48.269 | 48.885 | 35.828 |
| Alaska | 10.828 | 23.568 | 25.308 | 23.667 | 18.002 | 17.171 | 18.841 | 14.087 |
| Arizona | 8.275 | 29.047 | 33.729 | 32.922 | 23.852 | 23.343 | 23.641 | 17.327 |
| Arkansas | 13.057 | 36.497 | 35.773 | 34.985 | 28.537 | 26.746 | 27.505 | 21.579 |
| California | 91.797 | 225.894 | 202.749 | 202.843 | 154.574 | 145.410 | 153.592 | 113.867 |
| Colorado | 31.729 | 63.474 | 64.257 | 62.139 | 47.308 | 44.270 | 46.378 | 34.479 |
| Connecticut | 41.754 | 95.783 | 96.942 | 98.254 | 79.532 | 76.014 | 77.413 | 58.976 |
| Delaware | 5.542 | 17.384 | 15.189 | 15.172 | 11.957 | 12.573 | 13.016 | 10.436 |
| District of Columbia | 6.484 | 14.653 | 13.992 | 14.051 | 10.687 | 9.976 | 10.474 | 7.686 |
| Florida | 27.075 | 95.037 | 110.354 | 107.714 | 78.040 | 76.376 | 77.351 | 56.691 |
| Georgia | 21.407 | 75.141 | 87.252 | 85.164 | 61.702 | 60.387 | 61.158 | 44.823 |
| Hawaii | 2.137 | 4.652 | 6.023 | 6.027 | 6.107 | 5.416 | 6.159 | 4.514 |
| Idaho | 12.376 | 26.939 | 26.939 | 27.052 | 20.576 | 19.207 | 20.166 | 14.799 |
| Illinois | 114.565 | 237.236 | 232.865 | 238.712 | 185.684 | 160.191 | 167.458 | 124.493 |

| | Actual Allocations, FY2008-FY2014 | | | | | | | FY2015 Estimated Allocations |
| State | FY2008 Allocations: $1.98 Billion[a] (a) | FY2009 Allocations: $4.51 Billion[b] (b) | FY2010 Allocations: $4.51 Billion[c] (c) | FY2011 Allocations: $4.50 Billion[d] (d) | FY2012 Allocations: $3.47 Billion[e] (e) | FY2013 Allocations: $3.26 Billion[f] (f) | FY2014 Allocations: $3.39 Billion[g] (g) | FY2015 President's Budget Request: $2.55 Billion[h] (h) |
|---|---|---|---|---|---|---|---|---|
| Indiana | 51.872 | 103.609 | 104.151 | 102.749 | 80.006 | 72.374 | 75.820 | 56.367 |
| Iowa | 36.762 | 67.803 | 67.803 | 68.137 | 54.813 | 51.292 | 53.735 | 39.948 |
| Kansas | 17.031 | 45.349 | 41.757 | 42.327 | 32.160 | 31.397 | 31.019 | 23.526 |
| Kentucky | 27.230 | 68.353 | 57.742 | 58.335 | 46.423 | 43.483 | 48.288 | 36.372 |
| Louisiana | 17.494 | 57.196 | 51.870 | 53.164 | 43.422 | 40.864 | 42.062 | 33.869 |
| Maine | 26.815 | 49.457 | 54.309 | 53.539 | 39.982 | 37.414 | 39.195 | 29.139 |
| Maryland | 31.971 | 101.296 | 82.002 | 85.523 | 69.790 | 70.390 | 68.513 | 53.947 |
| Massachusetts | 82.797 | 162.981 | 175.524 | 175.178 | 132.731 | 132.256 | 140.014 | 103.857 |
| Michigan | 108.770 | 222.412 | 233.524 | 228.294 | 173.450 | 165.582 | 165.444 | 118.845 |
| Minnesota | 78.363 | 144.528 | 144.528 | 145.241 | 116.839 | 109.335 | 114.541 | 85.153 |
| Mississippi | 14.670 | 39.011 | 39.661 | 38.834 | 31.591 | 29.313 | 30.120 | 23.500 |
| Missouri | 45.762 | 103.541 | 95.257 | 95.596 | 68.231 | 66.553 | 70.882 | 51.215 |
| Montana | 14.517 | 31.598 | 31.598 | 31.730 | 24.135 | 22.529 | 23.654 | 17.358 |
| Nebraska | 18.180 | 39.573 | 39.573 | 39.738 | 30.226 | 28.214 | 29.623 | 21.739 |
| Nevada | 3.887 | 13.643 | 15.841 | 15.462 | 11.203 | 10.964 | 11.104 | 8.138 |
| New Hampshire | 15.672 | 34.112 | 34.112 | 34.255 | 26.055 | 24.321 | 25.536 | 18.739 |
| New Jersey | 76.865 | 166.690 | 177.196 | 180.991 | 136.746 | 124.480 | 124.570 | 91.267 |

| State | Actual Allocations, FY2008-FY2014 | | | | | | | FY2015 Estimated Allocations |
|---|---|---|---|---|---|---|---|---|
| | FY2008 Allocations: $1.98 Billion[a] (a) | FY2009 Allocations: $4.51 Billion[b] (b) | FY2010 Allocations: $4.51 Billion[c] (c) | FY2011 Allocations: $4.50 Billion[d] (d) | FY2012 Allocations: $3.47 Billion[e] (e) | FY2013 Allocations: $3.26 Billion[f] (f) | FY2014 Allocations: $3.39 Billion[g] (g) | FY2015 President's Budget Request: $2.55 Billion[h] (h) |
| New Mexico | 10.360 | 24.901 | 22.355 | 22.448 | 17.074 | 15.938 | 16.734 | 12.280 |
| New York | 250.974 | 475.935 | 479.526 | 495.801 | 375.710 | 350.169 | 366.843 | 272.722 |
| North Carolina | 37.730 | 123.243 | 109.339 | 111.263 | 83.011 | 87.702 | 88.271 | 70.719 |
| North Dakota | 15.770 | 34.325 | 34.325 | 34.469 | 26.218 | 24.473 | 25.695 | 18.856 |
| Ohio | 101.350 | 220.588 | 223.108 | 225.398 | 165.463 | 144.794 | 154.314 | 110.886 |
| Oklahoma | 15.729 | 49.007 | 47.902 | 47.717 | 36.094 | 35.955 | 37.147 | 29.813 |
| Oregon | 24.591 | 45.355 | 45.355 | 45.579 | 36.666 | 34.311 | 35.945 | 26.722 |
| Pennsylvania | 134.810 | 274.925 | 282.279 | 280.478 | 209.548 | 190.810 | 203.071 | 146.492 |
| Rhode Island | 13.629 | 30.209 | 29.666 | 29.790 | 23.241 | 23.976 | 23.813 | 17.824 |
| South Carolina | 13.590 | 47.702 | 47.311 | 46.909 | 36.270 | 38.335 | 38.825 | 28.455 |
| South Dakota | 12.808 | 27.878 | 27.878 | 27.995 | 21.293 | 19.877 | 20.869 | 15.315 |
| Tennessee | 27.584 | 73.723 | 72.092 | 71.595 | 55.405 | 56.856 | 58.040 | 45.524 |
| Texas | 45.044 | 158.110 | 183.593 | 179.200 | 129.832 | 127.064 | 128.686 | 94.316 |
| Utah | 14.745 | 32.094 | 32.094 | 32.228 | 24.513 | 22.882 | 24.025 | 17.631 |
| Vermont | 11.747 | 25.568 | 25.568 | 25.675 | 19.529 | 18.230 | 19.140 | 14.046 |
| Virginia | 38.944 | 118.084 | 100.856 | 102.839 | 80.436 | 78.971 | 81.877 | 64.211 |
| Washington | 40.450 | 74.603 | 74.603 | 74.971 | 60.310 | 56.437 | 59.124 | 43.955 |

| | Actual Allocations, FY2008-FY2014 | | | | | | | FY2015 Estimated Allocations |
| | | | | | | | | |
| State | FY2008 Allocations: $1.98 Billion[a] (a) | FY2009 Allocations: $4.51 Billion[b] (b) | FY2010 Allocations: $4.51 Billion[c] (c) | FY2011 Allocations: $4.50 Billion[d] (d) | FY2012 Allocations: $3.47 Billion[e] (e) | FY2013 Allocations: $3.26 Billion[f] (f) | FY2014 Allocations: $3.39 Billion[g] (g) | FY2015 President's Budget Request: $2.55 Billion[h] (h) |
|---|---|---|---|---|---|---|---|---|
| West Virginia | 17.935 | 40.584 | 38.884 | 39.047 | 29.700 | 27.723 | 29.108 | 21.361 |
| Wisconsin | 70.538 | 130.096 | 130.096 | 130.738 | 105.172 | 98.417 | 103.103 | 76.650 |
| Wyoming | 5.903 | 12.850 | 12.850 | 12.904 | 9.815 | 9.162 | 9.619 | 7.059 |
| Total | 1,977.027 | 4,476.302 | 4,476.302 | 4,494.258 | 3,437.068 | 3,248.193 | 3,370.409 | 2,507.400 |

**Source:** The Department of Health and Human Services (HHS) provided data on final regular fund allocations for FY2008 through FY2014 (columns (a) through (g)). Allocations to the states include tribal allotments, and FY2015 estimates assume that approximately 0.5% of the total would be set aside for the territories.

a. In FY2008, the funds that ordinarily would have been set aside for leveraging incentive and REACH grants—approximately $26.7 million—were distributed together with the formula grants. This increased the total amount allocated to the states compared to FY2007 despite the similar appropriation levels, and meant that distributions were calculated under the "new" LIHEAP formula.

b. Congress appropriated approximately $4.5 billion for LIHEAP as part of a continuing resolution (P.L. 110-329). Of this amount, $840 million was allocated under the "new" LIHEAP formula, with the remainder allocated according to the proportions of the "old" LIHEAP formula.

c. In FY2010, Congress appropriated the same amount for LIHEAP regular funds as it had in FY2009—approximately $4.5 billion—with the same division of funds between "old" and "new" formulas (P.L. 111-117). Although FY2010 LIHEAP funds were divided between the "old" and "new" formula in the same way as FY2009, the awards to the states are different because the formula factors were updated in April 2009.

d. The FY2011 Department of Defense and Full-Year Continuing Appropriations Act (P.L. 112-10) included an across-the-board rescission of 0.2% for discretionary accounts. This reduced the LIHEAP regular fund appropriation from approximately $4.51 billion to $4.50 billion. In addition, unlike appropriations in most years, HHS did not set aside funds for leveraging incentive and REACH grants, and instead included these funds in the formula grants to the states, bringing the total distributed to $4.49 billion.

e. The FY2012 Consolidated Appropriations Act (P.L. 112-74) included an across-the-board rescission of 0.189% that reduced the total available to $3.47 billion. Of the amount appropriated, $497 million was distributed according to the "new" LIHEAP formula and the remainder according to the proportions of the "old" LIHEAP formula. In addition, the law provided $3 million for training and technical assistance.

f. In FY2013, Congress enacted a full-year continuing resolution funding LIHEAP (and most other federal programs) at FY2012 levels (P.L. 113-6). While LIHEAP was funded at $3.472 billion in FY2012, a series of deductions meant that the total available for LIHEAP in FY2013 was $3.255 billion.

g.  The FY2014 regular fund appropriation for LIHEAP (P.L. 113-76) was reduced by 1% ($34.245 million) due to a transfer of funds within HHS, bringing the amount available to $3.390 billion. HHS did not distribute leveraging incentive and REACH grants, and it increased the territorial allocation from 0.134% of total funds to 0.500%. Of the amount distributed to states and tribes by formula ($3.370 billion), $491 million was distributed according to the "new" formula and the remainder according to the proportions of the "old" formula.

h.  The President's FY2015 budget would provide a total of $2.550 billion for LIHEAP regular funds. Of this amount, $366 million would be distributed according to the "new" formula, and the remainder, $2.184 billion, according to the "old" formula proportions. The proposal would set aside $27 million for leveraging incentive and REACH grants and $3 million for training and technical assistance.

# Author Contact Information

Libby Perl
Specialist in Housing Policy
eperl@crs.loc.gov, 7-7806